To Steve & Joanne

A Book of
Poems

Len J

DECAMEROONED

LEN GERMINARA

Edited by Sarah D. Oktay

"Buckley" – Published in *The Boston Literary Journal*, June 2020 as "Buckley, His Name Had We Kept Him"
"To the Last Ball Dropped" – Published in *More Than Enough Writings* from the SPC, 2022
"Fire Season" – Published in *Poetry Town/Worcester Magazine*, 2021
"Benign Canid" aired on WCAI Poetry Sunday 2022

ISBN: 978-1-7341378-3-5

Published in the U.S. by Viola Road Press.

Dedication

To my wife, Dr. Sarah Oktay, ILYSCB

Author's Note and Acknowledgments

Decamerooned is a collection of poetry comprised of 100 poems separated into ten sections that were crafted for Sacramento Poetry Center (SPC) workshops held in the isolation of Zoom room gatherings.

The author wishes to express his gratitude and appreciation to the facilitators of the various SPC writing groups and their participants. If it was not for them and the Zoom readings that sprang up overnight during COVID, I believe my outcome would have been very different. I also want to thank Sarah Oktay for her editorial and production work on this book.

Table of Contents

One 1

    Content... 2

    Just So 3

    Cinquain Kept a Rolling all Night Long 5

    Eastham Friday Night..................................... 7

    Horseshoe Crabs 8

    Shorebird Monitoring 10

    Day After Christmas #64................................ 11

    Savages... 12

    Petrichor.. 13

    Snippet 14

Two 15

    My Heart (ILYSCB)..................................... 16

    Soldier On.. 18

    Thinking of Hugh....................................... 19

    Trout Mask Replica 20

    To the Last Ball Dropped 21

    Benign Canid 23

    A Brief Vacation 25

    Mazel... 27

Just Last Week 28

From 120 Viola 29

Three 30

It was Raining When We Left CA 10/31 31

Coalinga 32

Waiting on a Credible Offer 34

Showing the House 36

House Not Home 38

Almont CO 39

(   ) 40

My Last Day of Work 1/26/20 41

Sample Size 42

First Order of Business 44

Four 45

Snoozing On the Couch 46

At the Edge of the Hockomock Swamp 47

Psithurism 48

3 AM Wake Up Call 49

Fall Asleep in Your Favorite Chair 51

Bar Hopping 52

Untitled 54

Frankly...55

The Place Doesn't Exist..56

Cold Comfort..57

Five 59

Portraits 60

Waif...62

Rolling Thunder...63

Instant Sis..64

Nutmeg...65

Grandmother's Stew...66

Lower Case b 67

Live Like someone Left the Gate Wide Open...........68

Pardoned..69

Wine List..70

Six 71

Let's get Wet 72

Antihistamine 73

Hanging Out at the Pool 74

The Green Has a Windmill..75

Savor...76

Buckley 77

Fire Season 79

Cupboard's Bare 81

Just Saying 82

Capital Projects 83

Seven 84

Water Ceremony 85

4 AM Walking the Dogs 86

Four feet to the Ceiling Happy 87

Cleaning My Brushes 88

I Got You 89

Restless Ellie / Valentines Weekend 2021 90

Superbowl 55 91

That's the Ticket – for Joe and Kamala 92

Never Mind the Bullock 94

Up Puppy 96

Eight 97

Decamerooned 98

Siege 100

Joe's Last Days in CA 102

Joe's Library 103

Eastham Beltane 104

The Desired Effect 105

All Good 106

Spot me a fiver 108

Trivial Apprehensions 110

Slam Haiku 111

Nine 112

In Different 113

White Lie 114

Just Time 115

How'll 116

Defied – for Zeus 117

Knell 119

Inured 120

For Dick Archer 121

His Poetry like Jimson Weed 122

Calliope Music 123

TEN 124

CODA 125

Contemplation 127

The Lost 128

Breaking it Down 130

Oran 131

Under an Opossum Moon 132

Reference Desk 133

Ry 134

Miscalculated 135

Certain at Curtains 136

About the Author 137

One

Content

Brief word before we begin
regarding language
    This is a warning

Any and all subjects
may be touched upon

Language will occur

Harbor no illusions
We aim for art
both
are subjective
and not always pretty
or our aim accurate

We welcome all
    We are not age
appropriate

If it's mean
or gratuitous
it's not welcome
    At all

We hold fast to
a Bourbon Street mantra
Be nice
or go home
    We mean it

Repeated use of small
words to advance
your point
may precipitate
someone handing you
a dictionary

That I think
should cover it

Just So

His portrait hangs
on the wall
to the right
of my desk
for just a few
days more
We share
      just this

A place all our own
we had but briefly
when we were
riding high

These are my last days
      on this crest
in my fortress of stoicism

Headed someplace
new

I've written an Ode
because I was asked to
so
I won't forget it

No matter where I sit
I'll be there
Still riding high
Contented scribbling
In front of the window
so
I can see anyone coming

Two doors
at opposite ends that

I might make my escape
should anyone initiate
an unwanted intrusion

Because I don't want to
talk about it

Cinquain Kept a Rolling all Night Long

(won)
Right now
We are one voice
The plague has got to go
No amount of magic thought will help
Now write

(too)
Dumb struck
Drop dead Gorgon
She does not like my face
Expect she won't be the last
Cancelled

(tree)
Plant me
Nice place you know
Return me to stardust
Water me liberally please
Thank you

(faux)
Unreal
The way you roll
Tell your story walking
You will not be missed – goodbye
Get out

(fie)
Ew – gross
I cannot look
Delicate Sensibilities
I turn and walk away
Head down

(sex)
Springtime
Ready to bloom
There is hope for us all
In spite of all evidence
I hope

Eastham Friday Night

There's a cricket in the wall
close to my right ear

Or
my tinnitus
has become more pronounced

I have a nagging suspicion
I'm forgetting someone
or something

This bow around my finger
makes zipper work
problematic

I'll need to pee
            eventually
Again

I have a pill box
to help me
track my daily doses

Had

My doctor gave me a shot
of cortisone
in my aching hip

Couple of Gummies
Martini
and I'm ready

for a backyard
lounge chair
harvest moon and
a smile from you

Horseshoe Crabs

We citizen scientists
Convinced field work
is something
we'd like to experience

Gather at 3 AM
on the incoming tide

to compile data
at the behest
of a local scientist

Neptune sets teeth
Nor and east

Cold wet   steel
yourselves
for this excursion

The doctor tells us
No data is data
          counting down
                    another species'
                              extinction
Let us begin
we're wasting time

We take temperature readings
note wind speed and direction
date...time....etc.

Set quadrants
Write zero
over and over

Cold – wet – a little depressed
On an open expanse of beach

In chest waders

Weak bladder
The bane
Your Waterloo

What do you doo

Shorebird Monitoring

I heard of you
that spring I worked
in Mr. Rogers' neighborhood
Massachusetts Ave.
The wild west end

Facing open ocean
      haulout for seals

Nesting ground for American oystercatchers
and piping plovers

We staked out those grounds
Fenced them in
So cars would not drive
                        right through

That never really works
There's always a dog
a football to toss
the remnants of lunch

One flip-flop

Sometimes it takes an anarchist
Someone to hold up the tide
      or a mirror

They are few and far between
Only here
for a short time

Buried in an unmarked grave
Somewhere you cannot drive to

Appreciated
Only after they are gone

Day After Christmas #64

Post Solstice
right for pre-spring
reconnoiter

Trees stripped bare
         expose paths to water

Where you'll be
         pre-spawn
made obvious

Moleskin and camera
ruck sack and
fishing gear
to prepare
for
pre-dawn
or sunset
situations

Blackberry sirens
Chanting green briar

Sublimation
hold me tight

while I write
poems
full of promise

in spite another
year of COVID

Savages

"... the merciless Indian Savages, whose known rule of warfare, is an undistinguished destruction, of all ages, sexes and conditions."
-United States Declaration of Independence

It will never be enough
No salvation will be found

The best you can hope for
A measured truce

This is the toll Empire takes
The written is indelible
immutable
As it well should be

History is a winding road
that leads back to you

All your atrocities

Speak these errant histories
All the unspeakable horrors

Lest you forget

The you   the us   the shame

Write that down
Pray
there is no judgement to follow

Or hell
beyond this

Petrichor

I wake with a book
pasted to my head

having fallen asleep
            two paragraphs into
Somerset Maugham's
Rain

A story I return to often
during droughts

Read as an incantation
carried into dreams

In the hopes I'll awaken
to drumming on the roof

What is that quiet smell
Precursor
to prayers answered

Or an indication
that no one is listening

Snippet

She asks
Do you think you'll ever
wear pants again

He ignores her
        for the moment

Caught up
on a horrible memory
Something odiferous
he'd rather forget

Turns on the radio
hoping for

Wait
Wait
Don't Tell Me

She pulls a package
of tart candy
from nowhere
like a character
in a Faulkner novel

He says
Pants are
overrated

Why do you ask

Two

15

My Heart (ILYSCB)

It's something like
a vestigial appendage

My need to begin the day
before the sun comes up

I do it in celebration
another day above ground

There are dogs to be fed
A cat as well

My wife values that last hour
before the morning comes

The day begins
with as little din
as possible

She gets nuzzles from all
and we're off

There is the backyard relief
Dishes of kibble

I make the coffee
Have a cup
Put the rest in a thermos
for Sarah
when she gets up

The dogs look forward
to what comes next
        The cat could care less

The young pup
has learned to bring his leash
The older guy
hasn't needed one
for years

We drive to a spot
where they can run

      Every day

There are treats
For the dogs   after

A smoothie for me
Coffee for her

We discuss the day to come
      Every day

Soldier On

Do not O wake
Make sure you
take the stairs
        correct in your posture

Slow moving shoal

Holdfast
the handrails

Your hip feels fine
at this moment

(it's sure to be fleeting)

Ice the knees each evening
        Gummies too
                Grab the heating pad

A preemptive strike

Actually
Terms of surrender

Thinking of Hugh

Every now and then
I'll come across an old recording
quite by accident

Bill Evans
Sunday at the Village Vanguard
maybe

Or searching for something
of you
while you were here
        Now gone
a whole year

of forever's

Blue
you're always
around the corner
        Butterfly
painted on the palm of your hand

I need that brother
        Sorry it took me so long
to write it out loud

Trout Mask Replica

There in orbit
To the left of Sirius
I reach out

Confirm your presence
in my firmament

I'm spinning Captain Beefheart's
Moonlight on Vermont

Responding to a writing prompt
based on a poem by Neruda

How he howled at the satellite of love

Raising my voice in unison
All the while
railing at the failings
of my fists

Gnarled testament that
Even victories
have a cost

You can count
on one hand

To the Last Ball Dropped

Arturo somnambulated
to the Mr. Coffee
as if his slippers bore him
on a lazy Susan

On his fourth rotation
past the island
Arturo grabbed a cup
On the fifth
he poured

He skipped cream and sugar
Certain the refrigerator
more than he could bear

On the sixth spin of the cycle
he got off
the Merry Go Round

Joined his wife on the porch
where she sat wrapped in silence
two German shepherds at her feet
a faraway look in her eyes

The coffee was weak
the last they had
it had to do

As if a command has been uttered
both dogs stand

Arturo and the Mrs. rose to go as well
Not a word between them

His mug in his right hand
She takes his left

The last morning
coming up over the Elk Mountains

without a sound

Benign Canid

3 feet proceeds me
most mornings

Leaves me scat
ghosts my track

Seldom seen more
than hind end

On purpose
        I suppose

That he rarely
ranges far
or wide

leads me think
someone may be
feeding him

The way 3 feet pees
indicates he's
a she

She moves well
in spite
the bum leg   she wanders on

What's the average age
of a Cape Cod coyote

I wonder

How many more
walks together
of a morning
will we have

A Brief Vacation

Dam
at the Old Mill
New Marlborough MA
Watching the river flow
Sundown
and so on

Drive in any direction
Before long
it becomes
Ann Teakey
Furniture priced
for looking
not buying

Every block
on the main drag
has a dispensary

Book shops
Restaurants
and coffee shops
thoroughly
round out the fare

This is how we
celebrate birthdays
holidays

All manner
life's transitions
these COVID days

Nestled in some
backwoods cabin BNB

Well provisioned
Appropriate clothing

Books (for reading)
Dogs
and walking shoes

We want for nothing
            save
more time

Mazel

Toyed with the idea
of a fire last night
Didn't
Not yet

We've got
dog and cat
bed warmers
jockeying for the hot spots
        where we are not
                when it gets chill

We like this
Something Wicked This Way Comes
weather

Soups with potatoes and cabbage
Stacks of poetry to be read
        Fresh baked bread

Coffee   Copious amounts

After
is a walk
at low tide
through Salt Marsh

Mud funk
in a time of Foxfire
on the autumnal Equinox
in Muck boots

Just Last Week

S'mores morning ground cover
Swallows begin their reconnoiter

Something swirls underwater
completely immersed

Book of high quality
hand stitched
priceless

centuries old images
animated

Walk on water
Wade into scrub oak
Wash over me

Atlantic

Ansley in his boat
Nettles in his parlor
Blue saying "AH!"

My dog Jake
long gone
        here with me

Green light flash
Last light of sundown
Black-crowned night heron squawking
to the mud flat

From 120 Viola

Keep on
calling me
Laddie

I nay mind
          Dearie

We Scots
find a way
to make
pain sound
          cheery
It's what we do

Our craggy
nature   we

nay excuse
to offer

None
of any use any way

It's not   tough
we are
                    Stout
we are

If nothing more than
dust
We are

I'm good with that
               You?

Three

It was Raining When We Left CA 10/31

We ate at Denny's
our last day in California
We both ordered Grand Slam Breakfasts

Because it
was World Series week
        and we're making a home run

While waiting
We check our email
Scan the Facebook feed
Terribly metropolitan
Completely addicted

A pic pops up
of a dear pet pup
passed
on my hand-held device

Jake was a great dog
A "rescue"

These are tears to honor him

We'll turn east this morning
Route 58
towards the Mojave
We're south of Death Valley

These signs are warnings
or leftover
Halloween decorations

Coalinga

We take I 5 South
Moving back to Massachusetts
for my 64th birthday

Moving lock
stock (2 dogs and 1 cat)
The wife and I

Packed tight
in a Nissan Xterra

From Sacramento
on to Bakersfield

Its foggy on the roadside
       In our heads

These last few weeks have been
goodbyes and farewells

A blur we won't fathom
any time soon

We're nearing Santa Nella
The next four exits
offer access
to the Korean War Memorial

I think of my father – Angelo

The fog a familiar
arm on my shoulder
The sunbaked fields
look like an Xray image
of a cancerous lung

Coalinga smells
like it sounds
We pass through
doing 70 MPH

She puts Muddy Waters
on the CD player

We all growl
40 days
and 40 nights

We stop at a La Quinta
She says
That's Spanish for
right next door to a Denny's

This one is just off
Merle Haggard Drive

I wonder how we'll sleep tonight

Probably
like the dead

Waiting on a Credible Offer

We've been playing
pop goes the real estate market

Colored balls percolating
in a child's pull along toy

O asks
You want to go for a ride

She tells me
she's on fire

and even though
I'm no wanderer

the answer is always yes

regardless of viruses
mega-fires
distance
all day drives
all hindrances

because I'm a follower

and

it does get easier
        Google be praised

She no longer
drives one hand on the wheel
the other holding a map

Going 75 MPH
because that's the speed limit

Our animals are used to it
They look forward to the exotic jerky
available at every roadside stop

The hum of the tires on tarmac
A lullaby and a belly rub

Showing the House

Friday
we took it
on the heel and toe

Rough packed
the Subaru

Put the pups in back
and skedaddled

So
the real estate agent
can show the house .

We're gone to San
something or other

Booked a quaint BNB
by the bay
for the weekend

Going $4.59 a gallon
miles per hour
to Half Moon bay

Mid-morning
we hit sand
and funky shops
with hand painted signs

Tye-dyed geriatrics
Sidewalk cafes
Boutiques and bookshops

It was good
to feel the fog again

Leave the grind behind
if only
for a moment

House Not Home

The last night
we huddled
on the bare floor
in sleeping bags
with our two pets

The house empty
Our worldly possessions
gone on before us
The place
never really home
Just somewhere
to hang our hat
for a moment

We have some pictures
One or two
Facebook connections
little more

When we shut the door
we were already gone

Almont CO

Sunrise is delayed
in the Gunnison Forest

Sol climbs the Elk Mountains
slow

A glow before
full blown

It's mother shaking you awake
with promises of pancakes
maple syrup and bacon

Step out the back door
dog in tow

coffee steaming in your
favorite mug
        So much magic

Some days the back yard harbors
Mountain lions
or Mule Deer

waiting for the
what comes next

nary a sound between them

(   )

Edge of pond
Early morning

Place so quiet
first light
sneaks up on itself

A lone herring gull drops in
with a breeze

The water a welcome relief
from salt and sand
whatever else unwanted

She flutters and shudders
A fishy windsock
dancing a jig
to the approaching storm

Just below
a snapping turtle

My Last Day of Work 1/26/20

We are live outside the home
Police and investigators
are on the scene

100 yards from where we stand
someone who should not have had a gun
in one last rage against that
which his wife
could no longer cope with

Shot his son
Then himself

At about the same time
Kobe Bryant's
helicopter crashed
Killing all onboard

The 6 o'clock news this night
will lead with details
of the legend's death
The sad passing
of all on board

Flowers and cards
will be left at the scene

They'll be a brief mention
of the father and son
the mother's grief

Tomorrow comes quietly
a skunk's silhouette
Slinks through the shadows
unaware of the DOT van
its occupants
that do their work
without any fanfare

41

Sample Size

I've long found
myself at odds
with popular
opinion

I seek it

Find it suspect

I'll use as an example
the year
Go Set a Watchman
was published

O and I were meandering
across country
by auto

We noticed its prominent positioning
Front counter
of every bookstore
we visited

Bright shiny displays
heralding its arrival

Asked every bookseller
their opinion of it

To a person
they parroted
the New York Times
less than effusive review
published on its release

Second question
Have you read it
       The answer   no

Every bookseller across 21 states   we counted

First Order of Business

The notice is posted on social media
Mudslide warning

It's not even raining
But it's expected

These scarred hills
sluice into Berryessa
I don't wanna

So I get in my car
and go

Discretion
the better part of valor

These hills will be here
tomorrow

As they have been forever

Four

Snoozing On the Couch

My watch signals
how long
I've been sedentary

Wriggles on my wrist
swarm of whispering vipers
telling me

Time To Get Moving

The watch face screams
You've been sitting
over an hour

It's in cahoots with
my cell phone

Which in turn
tracks my banking

All my recent transactions
groceries and dispensaries
            My beating heart

informs me
how to get from
point A to B
Perfunctorily

In a voice
of my own choosing

We are no longer on speaking terms

It's no doubt
my fault

At the Edge of the Hockomock Swamp

Twilight
Place haunted
since time was new

Joe's Honda CVCC
chooses to break down here

Damned $500.00 beater
not worth the oil in the crankcase
or big enough
to sleep in

No service station for miles
Long stretch of coal black
Nowhere

One lone streetlight   flickering

This may be the night
King Phillip
returns from the dead
to avenge his brother
under a bigfoot moon

It would be
just Joe's luck

He should have tried harder
to make a go of it

Walking away never
solved anything

He did love her
        He thinks

Psithurism

I've picked out
the grove of elms

Stumbled upon it after
a first snow
some years ago

Far from any homes
or roads

I don't remember
how I got there
        or why

It's where I'd like to lie
when I die

Until then

I'll keep all my clocks
stopped
set at four and twenty
songbirds
Singing Buckley's *Last Goodbye*

I'll still hurt
as much
but I can sway with joy
Not rage
and that's enough

While I sit here
        Wondering why

3 AM Wake Up Call

Every molecule
now enemy
knows
efficacy fades

Finally dies
altogether

Gasping for air
awakened
        Muscle contraction

Bone break sneeze
Siren song
Oxycontin

Hoping spring
        Its attendant warmth
will kickstart this rickety
strawman
here among the walking dead
in my dreams

Waking the Dragon
Armageddon night-light

Face behind the face
in the bathroom mirror

Dragging us all
to Gethsemane

Cue the calliope music

Writing light verse
Rhyming carcinoma
with the color
of your eyes

For a poetry reading
in hell

Fall Asleep in Your Favorite Chair

Pot head so long
He worries not

Why he can't remember
what brought him
into this reoccurring dream
of a bar that closed in 98
Or the name of his cat

Tells the barflies
that surround him
at the rail
        I pay good money for that

Because everything hurts
when he stands or sits

Notes the pain's intensity
increases
no matter how
the day passes

Ticking clock
Running tab
Strumming fingers

Tells himself
One more for the road
then

Go home old fella

Bar Hopping

Blues going nowhere
Fast
and broke

Grab a schooner or two
at the Grog
on your way home
from work

Pay attention to the details pal
The barstools here
have bad intentions and
Debby over there
got the clap
and
Iris won't take
her teeth out
No matter the inducement

Just play pool – dummy
you'll be better off

Pony up
the buck and a quarter
if you want to shoot next

This is a faded memory
of a carefree existence
based on unrealistic
expectations up in flames

The same old
"it used to be better"
Crap that frustrated old men
have always muttered
on their way
to the Bay of Fundy

Untitled

What an age we live in
Predicted in the science fiction
we read as children

Even the surreal
becomes mundane
given the proper
repetition

Allow me to say

I am whelmed
Slightly

I'll remain here
as long as
it doesn't hurt
too much

Until then
there are books to read

Libraries Borges
imagined
infinite and connected

As for
the rocking chair rodeo
beckoning
With its BBQ's and Sunsets

I have one last request

Shut the door

Frankly

I don't recall
with any certainty
the day
you went bed-bug crazy

Because I choose not to

I'm sure life's pressures
weighed heavy

We've all been
a disappointment to someone
at some point in our life

It just is

I came across a picture
of we two
Faded proof we existed
somewhere   briefly
before you went away

never a word
in the intervening years

I'm still ok
with all of that

Mostly

Lenticular displays are created by placing a lens on top of a print, so that the image has an illusion of depth, or can change or move as the image is viewed from different angles.

The Place Doesn't Exist

Stool at the counter
Sits this howler monkey
of a Saturday passed
after

Banging cymbals
wash ashore screeches
bumper to bumper
Route 6 ambulance chasers

One after the other

I
Beseech thee succor
Tell the server
I will settle for ice water
and coffee
If they're out of hemlock

The hash is touted
Best on cape
It may cure or kill

The Latter might be a blessing quite frankly

Of no great import - see
I'm here for "The Best"
Bloody Mary on the cape

Fresh celery V8 revving
Cheese stuffed olives
Thick cut bacon choking
Cholula kissed Vodka
Chilled to perfection
I'll keep looking

Cold Comfort

Having spent some time
in rooms with no windows

Calling to the nurse
that does not hear

is not there
Just trying to do
the best she can

for Christ's sake

She knows I took
a laxative

and I'm entirely
unable to do this
by myself

I worry for my mother
because she's in
such a room at present

I call her
The calls often end in

Baleful whimperings
Through bit lips

Seldom does she
call me by my name

Remember the call
ten minutes later

The only solace
if it is
in fact
Solace

Is in the knowing
she thinks she's
at work

dad's on the way to
pick her up
and tomorrow
is Thanksgiving

Simpler this year
cause it's just

the two of them now

Five

Portraits

1.

I've read there
Told beforehand
You'll find your host
something of a dick

I did

In a dim and dusty
gin joint in Gloucester
he put on quite a show

Continued back at his uncle's house
Insulting his friend
in ways
I could only marvel at
        Ways I never would have thought of myself

Dick really doesn't begin to describe him

2.

The poet famous for his irascibility
did not discriminate the year we met

Survived his salvo
His dear wife
standing behind him
cheering me on
my ham-handed compliment

He took wrong

He called me late one night
Said

You get it
I'm sick
this isn't an act

Ever the optimist
I invited him back

Waif

Danni sat on the stairs
leading to Planet Records
Wearing cutoff jeans
Sex pistols t-shirt

Finally clean
and refreshed

She stayed with the Albino
last night
       She won't do that again

She's been a fixture
in Kenmore Square
for the past few weeks

A runaway
With a pixie hair cut
       Every street urchin loves her

She's 16

She won't say where she's from
She doesn't ever want to go back

or have a clue
where she's going

Rolling Thunder
An erasure for Robert Zimmerman

Ancient empty streets dreaming
Best thing he's
Ever seen

All the pretty people
Drinking

All alone
Must get stoned

Raining from the first
Dying there of thirst
In here

Saw it tangled up

Your loyalty
To me
The stars

Your dancing spell
Under it

Come in
From the storm
Stand inside my shoes

What a drag it is

Instant Sis

In the photo
she wears
a plastic beach bucket
for a hat

We are
brother and sister
Not yet double digits

Our connection to mum
Whose memory fades like denim

Static on the line

There are other photos
in the album

Polaroids taken at family events
picnics and amusement parks

Proof of days
well spent

Like ticket stubs kept
Old newspaper articles clipped
Other ephemera

Things we hope
to remember

Nutmeg

I remember the first time
I sat on my scrotum
accidently
       like it was yesterday

I was in the back of
Francine Salmon's
VW Rabbit

A screwed up
half wound stopwatch
at the start of a footrace

Yes
I'm aware of the Rabbit
irony

It's not funny
She's been permanently cock-eyed
ever since

My fahrvergnügen was
adversely effected for some time
as well

So
Here I sit on my
       Zoom- Zoom - Zoom
Fuzzy and out of focus
Having re-lived the event

Too many times to count

Grandmother's Stew

One Saturday
every spring
my father would secure my service

Ply me with breakfast
Pancakes and bacon   real maple syrup

In exchange for a date
with a shovel and hoe

Plant what was begun from seed
in my grandfather's basement

On tables
           below windows
that greet the sun
in just spring

Tomatoes and squash
Garlic and onions   Basil and marigolds etc.

Break the ground
Shake the clods
Stick your hands
in living soil

Ritual as old as living memory

All these years later
my back still aches

every time
I eat ratatouille

Lower Case b

He's measured the snow fall
for forty years
at an abandoned mine
in a place called Gothic

Yet the hook to the story
is the notion that he's a hermit
like Judd before him

The elevation is 13,000 ft
Most souls at elevation hibernate
He doesn't

He's been watching
Bollywood musicals
on video tape
Because he secretly
loves to dance

Plays cricket at elevation
in the summer
amongst the yellow-bellied marmots

A freezer full of ice cream from the third bowl
one of his many treasure troves

Simply put   He's got it all

For so many souls
The high country holds an allure

He went to Colorado for a summer
while in school
Stayed awhile
Then a little longer

As it turns out   forever
A fine fellow

barr none

Live Like someone Left the Gate Wide Open

Behind the green wall
a summer party is in full flower

Parents and children
In-Laws and Out laws

Everyone is wearing the latest pastel
      Sipping their favorite beverage

The passengers in my van
Children from the Boys and Girls Club

We drive by

Take notice
long before he's upon us

A gleaming white poodle
comes running through the privacy hedge
of his backyard

Tongue lolling
Ears flapping
Happy

Into
and under
the left wheel well

Nothing I could do about it

Pardoned

He died
in a locked from the inside
bathroom

Needle of a gauge
for mixing not fixing
Some smack and other props

It's where he worked

and if the works don't fit
He did not commit

Dig

He called someone in the audience
cock sucker

Busted over protestations
          from the audience member in question

Saying loud and proud

I am

The Bust destroyed Bruce
Never really worked again
NY revoked his cabaret card

Remember who it was
that spoke the truth
The first time you heard it
and why it's

Not always what you want to hear
Something to defend
Like life itself

Wine List

Young woman
Someone I've known
since she was little
            Now with a child all her own

Groan

Everything hurts
Here in bed I'll stay

Hoping for commiseration
She mentions dying as a possibility

I understand her pain

Right down to the dollars and cents

Debt collectors
still deal in the bones
of Thomas Paine
Who left unpaid
promissory notes
on two continents

Tell me dear heart

Who'll be holding the bill
when you check out

Six

Let's get Wet

She explained sublimation
the first morning we woke
on Folgers Marsh

Later
on a walk
our dog Jake
discovered a water snake
the size of a truck tire

He went to heel
we were taken aback

Without a camera

We vowed in that moment it would be the last time

We walked that property daily
for decades

Searching for flotsam in the wrack line
Fruiting bushes
Swirls of fish in the harbor

Antihistamine

Another morning dew
      Lemon yellow
           Seed slick
                Viscous kiss
Good morning

Trap door spiders wait in
fresh cut grasses
Proficient assassins
famished

Tom and his rafter
Strut and peck
Strut and peck
Strut

Joe
half asleep
Bow legged ambles
to the swimming pool
as if a siren is singing

He hasn't had his coffee
Won't acknowledge
anything but immersion
he heads for the pool

Until his toes get wet
none of this
exists

Hanging Out at the Pool

There are high bush blueberries
next to the aspen in the backyard
we may never taste

The catbirds are already
shaking the branches
          Leave messages of impudence
          on the lawn furniture

Chipmunks wait in the shadows
of this windfall habitat

A coterie of scurrying
engorged
bottom feeders in fur coats
and yellow sneakers

A turkey hen drops from an elm
Poults in tow
          Coyote wary

Sunset will bring the bats
They like our pool
We like their appetite

The chirring in the scrub
Whirring of the pool filter

A rumble of thunder

The Green Has a Windmill

Geographically remote spit of sand
Stomping ground for all manner
of eccentric

Lovely place with a
pirate back-story

What old folks used to call
Make do charm

Memory heavy on bluefish
Monday through Friday

Chowder
Saturday and Sunday   also bluefish

Candlelight flicker
when the power went out

Town meeting for governance
Concerts on the village green
Monday evenings June-September

There's a windmill in the center of town

Truth be told
There is no
Center of town

What the old folks used to call
Quaint

We call it home

Savor

You develop routines at the water's edge
to fit the tides

Note the seasons
for the fish
Where they feed

Watch the birds
like a hawk

Follow scat trails

because venison
is tasty

Scout the berry patches
Pick some *Salicornia*

Fox grape
for sure
Rose hips
a secret wish

Note how many bayberries it takes
to make one lumen live

Savor the moments
Then move on

Leave something for the next
Gather flotsam

Shop at the Take it or Leave it
Become as Epicurus suggested

Waste nothing

Buckley

Found a blue-black Labrador retriever
abandoned on the new year

Huddled around a garbage can
in a dog park

Obviously shell shocked
Howling terror and WTF in woof

I shared a look with my dog
that said
Let's help this poor son of a bitch out

It took some doing
        Fear like that
requires caution

My dog Swegen knows what to do
Never seen him falter
in a touchy Canid social encounter
        A true   Tich Not Hound

He wags
They wag back

This will be an understanding
forged in urine
licks and sniffs
The obligatory
submissive roll

Every move I make
reminds this poor soul
of the night just passed

I'll sit at a slight remove
Wait for him
to return from the hell of
being thrown away

The dogs
Tentatively at first
            begin to play

While the morning doves ask who-who-who

He comes around
quick as any infant
            Terror already forgotten

He sidles up to me
in the hope that I'll
pet him and tell him

It's ok — it's ok -- it's

Fire Season

We saw the first sparks
of this conflagration

No
We felt them

Wrapped in our predawn habits
Our morning walks

A dry storm
crackling static

Metallic taste
the dog felt it first

      A skittish reaction

We watched
      Waited for the patter
            that did not follow

While the etch-a-sketch
of a night sky
painted a triptych
of exclamation

We went on with our day

Labyrinth and compulsion
The sweep of feet

We've walked every day since
      months now
No end in sight

The only thing that remains
normal
The pre-dawn dark

There's comfort in that

Cupboard's Bare

Who was it crow
brought us as present
still warm from nest
one of seven

Trail of red

lead us back
where six remained
asleep
Adjusting to the sudden chill

Draw closed the curtain
Plucked angora and woven with a
dutiful mother's precision

Scene from a Jack London yarn

Just Saying

If I should
die at home

My own bed
Of my own volition

My last wish

Here's my list

Music played
as I slip away

Richard and Linda
Dimming of the Day

Dargai
Pour down like silver

Slow drip of
something soothing

A favorite
movie clip

Something from "The Departed"

I'd go quietly

Capital Projects

We installed solar power
Capital outlay
Prayer for a better world
Someday

Crew of ten do the work
The crew chief proclaims

You'll be creating
your own power

Which lifts our keel
unfurls our sails

Leaves us waiting at the dock
for the electrical inspector
before we can
flip the switch

Monday appointment
No show – call or explanation
Wednesday
No show – rescheduled due to heavy rain
Friday

I've a feeling of Déjà vu
There are turkey vultures
overhead
Portent of dread

A phone rings

The wait is over
Half an hour later
inspection completed

We are lit

Seven

Water Ceremony

Our dogs like
Great Pond
just fine in the morning

The confluence of water
            communal relationships

The sunrise crowd of dog walkers
are kind
All the dogs dig the water

There are benches
for the old H2O molecules

Like me

In the afternoon
the boys and I
head to the beach

First Encounter

Look for dead things
at the lee

Lift up the codium
See what lies under

Smolts and razors opened

Things to roll in
before an afternoon dip
dinner
                and a watercolor sunset

4 AM Walking the Dogs

My headlamp's light
follows the contour of the trail
to Laguna Creek
Particulates dance through the wash
Dense as Vesuvius

The beam hits red in the underbrush
where things are as scary
like Crazy Joe and his un-leashed dog

He lives around the corner
one cul de sac over
Tells me
I don't know how to control my dogs

I tell him

PUT YOUR DOGS ON A LEASH
PLEASE

Turn the beam from my lamp
level with his eyes
so he feels me

He's still talking
We never stop walking

I'm glad that's all it is

A moment better than caffeine
        It keeps us regular

Four feet to the Ceiling Happy

He is an echo
in the antechamber
that was the beach
of his youth

Many a night muttering
odes of joy

Body surfing
       Drooling

The *Salicornia* turning red
signaling scallop season

Never enough day
to satisfy him

It's hard to pinpoint
what he liked best back then
       everything was oyster

These days
he has a fireplace
Loves the hearth

Comforting voices
surround him

Puppy as companion
a favorite cat
that curls up next to him
Two humans
that love him   and CBDs

Cleaning My Brushes

I search him out
His favorite hideaway spots
      Every day since the first

So long now
it seems like time
in memoriam

We need not speak
      Rarely do

If then only
to murmur *I got you*
into his floppy ears

Twitch of hand
usually says all
that's needed

The only sound
The turning of the tide
      Contented sigh

This is me intentionally dreaming
      Wishing on Sirius
That we get back to the
land of the bean and cod together

That he might feel
that kind of puppy
happy once more
Before sunset

I Got You

Here in your
own bed

Snug
in familiar
sights and sounds

Your place
all you've ever known

I got you

Close your eyes
like so many times before

Dream of the day
to come

Go ahead
I'll be right here with you

I love you

Restless Ellie / Valentines Weekend 2021

Between the door and dogs
there is a swath
unknown to my feet
          terrain of a
rented camper

Two nights in the Sierra foothills
Our COVID anniversary getaway

My wristwatch is a nightlight
When I twist out of bed

my phone becomes a GPS
for sleepwalkers with restless legs

When our dogs snore
I play it by ear

It's all good
          All right
                    It's OK

Fall back to the sleep
to the sound of
rain on the aluminum roof
of this Airstream B&B Atheneum

With my world all around me

Superbowl 55

There's dragon breath
crawling along Jacinto Creek this morning

The ground underfoot
foul smelling
A viscous morass

It's always like this
after a fog in a dog park

We have business here
It won't take long for
highway 99 to wake up
Shoo us away

So many used food wrappers
air borne

Ancient ritual
Absolute imperatives
       Whatever you might call it

The dogs do
We go home

Get ready for the big game
      The puppy bowl
          scrabble
               beer and nachos
my favorite holiday tradition

Ignoring Tom Brady

That's the Ticket – for Joe and Kamala

The Blues got the leg of my jeans
in a twist

Persistent nuisance
chewing socks and
loose shoelaces
        Like texts from Joe and Kamala

A high-pitched beehive
resting on my right shoulder
Meandering down to my knees
        Two puddles of sulphur on the boil

I got the kind of Blues
that makes overmedication
almost inevitable

Oh
for the comfortable surroundings
and warm narcotic drip
Edward G. Robinson got
in *Soylent Green*
on his way out the door

Which will one day
feel like a long-ago dream
to you who will inherit
this dumpster fire of a world

I got the Blues
for herd immunity

Already overcome with Mad Cow disease
in the White House

This isn't TV or a bad dream

This is it
which runs downstream
Blue is the only choice
Vote

Never Mind the Bullock

We've added a life
Pup eight weeks old

Another working dog
Companion for our Doodle
          Irritation for our cat

For the foreseeable future
a puddle possibility

Trip and fall obstacle
to be sure

He's a chewer
Learning his body
in romps around
the yard
for the joy of stretching limbs
Testing boundaries

The disappointment of glass doors
closed
Gravity of stairs
Taste of bitter apple
A blooper reel per second

Naps

          Lots of naps

We've reacquired a type
of Tourette's
last exhibited
eleven years ago

Not profane
Emphatic   Nos!

Everything will be examined
Tiny razor-sharp teeth
Puppy breath
Wet nose on glass

We'll be sleep deprived   a tad cranky
and keeping an eye on the cat

Up Puppy

Up with the puppy
we got to keep moving

Trip on something
I should recognize

It's moist
Obviously misshapen

Hope it's nothing
O holds dear

I'm not saying
this pup is on my last nerve

Or that he'll be
the death of me

But I'm sure
I'd never hear the end of it

Should anything
happen to him

while in my charge
I'd wager

Eight

Decamerooned

Joe and Madge
are talking about squirrels again
      Constant source of consternation
They've shared videos
with the other
depicting ingenious catapults
that can launch
those pesky scamps
clear into another
time zone

Not that Havaheart
bait and switch BS

      Joe and Madge
      have worked in the field
      doing tick studies

Seen the snakes lined up
at the rabbit crates gates

A serpentine line
cued up for take out

Have felt the hearts beat
unbelievably fast and burst

It's last tremens
move from the hand
up your arm
Settles in your soul

Coughing
My compromised health
may keep me sequestered
During this plague's duration

COVID is out there
waiting

Siege

Dust up at the bird feeder
Bastogne redux

Fuzzy Fuhrer
shoots Joe a Zieg Hiel!
with his middle finger

Squirrel I thought male
        Two rows of angry red
        Swollen nipples

Look in her eyes
that says lock jaw
Jackass   gird your loins

Itititititit

Terms were discussed
pretty sure
promises were made

Can't say I'm confident
        she's appeased

This is not about
gender identification
or
whatever it is
put the bug
up her bushy butt
and
pardon me

I'm just getting up to speed
On they and them
          Always have been
a step or two behind

I'm compelled to ask
What does
Itititititit mean

Them never saw this coming
          Best case scenario
She'll/they'll go on
about they day
Them will wander away

On second thought
          Itititititit me

Nuts
To you

Joe's Last Days in CA

Joe woke in his back yard
Sun itch on his neck

Coffee gone cold
        Book on his chest
                Glasses on the ground

Discombobulated

While somewhere
beyond his eyes acuity

one dusty old cat
sits ambush in the azaleas
squirrel on her mind

Wind kicks up
Rustles the chimes
hung in the redwoods

Rattles her resolve
Slinks off self-satisfied
nonetheless

Joe's Library

Joe's settling in
>   New place
Something he's done
often

He marvels at the ephemera
survived decades of
rough packing
diffident unloading
>   life's black and white
>   back and forth
>   Rubik's Cube

Stare into the etching
hanging by the window
An archway
Turin in the distance
that goes on

Labyrinth   Ecco
Footfall on wet marble
>   Well-worn steps
Women on the way
to the market

Oak bookcases
Tumescent fruit

Sip rye whiskey
in front of an electric
fireplace
Backgammon after dinner

Could this have
any permanence   like a book

Eastham Beltane

Joe's planting cucumbers
Whistling first day of May ditties

Naked old man
refrain
hedge trimming
butt naked

Avoid ladders until
long after sunset

Watch where you're stepping

You'll not want to know
how Joe furrows his rows

Seed dropped
straight and true

Woodpecker precision

Come on
October sunset's diminution

Fare thee well
summer
its visitors

Etm.

The Desired Effect

Joe is headed to the Post Office
when he's alerted
to the sound of
dogs whimpering
that are not with him

It's just the wind
blustering through
his creaky old loaf
of an SUV

He pulls over at the donut shop
Ostensibly to get coffee
But also
to confirm
it's the wind

When
All in a whoosh
Like a bullet missing – just
He realizes

That   yes
the right mix
of CBDS and THC
In his morning dose
does...

Joe doesn't remember why
he's headed to the Post Office

All Good

It was the pearlescent shank
of the early morning

That ravenous hole
between the first Schlitz
and putting pen
to paper

Joe
already cigar infused
Not terribly inclined
towards anything

at all past this

Leans back in his chair
looks down to the mutt
at his feet

Little drool and a fart
let's Joe know
they're both
still amongst the living

It's all good

Signals
Time for a walk
to the beach

First an ear twitch
Then a tail swish
They're off

Whistling past the redwing
Blackbirds in the *Baccharis*

All the way
to the first splash

Spot me a fiver

I've been sleeping in
now that the weather grows cold
Which throws the whole household
into a tither

They bear with me
My warmth and snuggle
more than welcome

I'm up briefly
at 12, 2, and 4

The cat
ever hoping to get fed
Waits in ambush
by the entrance to the WC
The dogs don't move a muscle

With any luck
I'm going back to bed

If the cat gets pushy
I may pee on her head
at 12:05, 2:05, or 4:05

The way back always
an obstacle course

Bones tossed from the
        tower of babble and kibble

Digital clock
Red eyed and malevolent

Someone
wake me up
at 5

Trivial Apprehensions

It simmers in dank recesses
Rank and indiscriminate
Dirty bath linen
So many messes

Leaves smudges on the walls
Takes phone calls
Never leaves messages

It's dirt and hair
Immune to vacuum cleaners

Tomato soup stains
On a white shag carpet
    Snot on velour

No solvent can quiet remove it
We've searched for professional help
So far
    All have declined   Damn it

I'm at my wit's end
And I have little to lend

This well may be my undoing

These are the striations
2 dogs one cat

Two cooks
That hate to do dishes

They all need cleaning
    Before we sell our home

Because time runs out and
We must be going
These things need doing

Slam Haiku

Climate change ya know
That's what really matters
If you have children

Nine

In Different

Here's to the deluded
      I hope you're happy

A salute
to the self-important
      Go hug yourself

Goodbye to the dissatisfied
We hardly knew ye

Can I get a woot woot
for the defeated

The ones that never had a chance
from the get-go

Thoughts and prayers
for those with dumb luck

Eternal indigestion and anal warts
for opponents
of legalized abortions

God Damn it

Set 'em up Joe
Raise a glass
to the last inane moment

Capture it in a flash
of the fuck we don't have left to give.

White Lie

I never bought the line
America the great

Land of the free
Home of the brave

Good and bright people
Moral and empathetic

All that bullshit

I stopped saluting the flag
long ago

Never became a Boy Scout
        Wouldn't be a Webelo

America
You're a lie
You may have been
Great and good
Once
For a moment

I'm searching for evidence
most of my life
with nothing
to show for it

Just Time

There was time
World still wild

Lurking menace
in the coal bin
Monster in the furnace

Saturday was Tarzan
swinging from the jungle
gym in the schoolyard

Every kid in the
neighborhood
knew the call

Lunch was a Fluffernutter
potato chips and farm fresh milk
all mashed together

Sunday was fishing
Schwinn bicycles and
skinny dipping in the town reservoir

late at night enough
to get away with it

It has always been
a bit dangerous
and ridiculous

Because the ones
making the decisions
are idiots

You know
us

How'll

There's a manic dog barking
red hobgoblins
in the background
of this revelry

It's making my remaining hair
bow-legged

Astrid Gilberto earworms
my noggin
tickles my fancy
on the radio
way down on the dial

These poems cum and go
tonight

Time is not a melting clock
You're not punching
         Really

A Kung fu movie star
In a tough part of town
         You
Want to kick someone
Goofy while

Wearing plaid polyester pants
Platform boots and a flaming red
Wide brimmed fedora
         Just for the hell of it

It's been that kind of day

Defied – for Zeus

Last year
Two words combined
That defy definition or
Understanding

I cannot begin to consider
A year in review

Won't do it
No thank you

This machine smokes out
apathy and dereliction
with Ginger Baker beats
already banging
on drums unborn

Makes me want to holla
Welcome to the Renaissance

Last year
is a tomorrow poet today

The day after is anybody's guess
         Keep throwing hands in the air

It's a blur of beams
circular rotation

Feel the hum
Steel yourself

Leave history to Herodotus brother
          You
write the verse
that heralds peace

Let the folks that think
the plague is past us
go downtown
with Darwin's blessings
Probably just as well
Wholesale cuts are coming

Carpe Diem

Knell

Berm between us
Sheltered harbor
Breached

Foghorn moan
          All morning

Black-crowned night heron croak
Wind and a prayer

Fiddler's roll
Tidy up
High tide comes

Skedaddle

Gulls crack
Spider crabs

Drop them
death spiral

Slack tide
Horseshoes emptied
Red knot absent

Inured

I wonder
how in touch
with our feelings
we will be
if it gets as bad
as has been predicted
for better than
a half century

Will we ponder
our chakras
Forgive our debtors
Sit shiva

Pray
for the coming of the light

And what of poetry

How does
profoundly hungry
alter one's perspective
if you know
this could have
all been avoided

For Dick Archer

It doesn't take long
to make a place yours
the older you get

Experience teaches
eschew place settings
for eight
there's just you

A few plates and utensils
A glass or two
will do

Space is overrated
with its need to be filled
with stuff
that will need dusting

At heights beyond reach
or aspiration

Screw it

So much simpler
when you realize

Life is a diminution
and here's not so bad

The table and chairs
Sturdy and serviceable
The murphy bed comfortable

This will do

His Poetry like Jimson Weed

I found this abandoned bindle
in the Bridgewater Triangle
last night

It had
Metacomet   etched into   the handle

I hadn't dreamt myself in a
Preston Sturges movie
since I don't know when
        and the idea of Veronica Lake…

All this pervaded my dreams
after hearing you read your poetry
last night
Robert

I wrote this down during
a virtual field trip
online
this morning

No
Spoke it into my phone
actually

Does that make me a spoken word poet
or a rhapsode
that's been hoboing
in my sleep

Calliope Music

The roller coaster at Nantasket Beach
Was a wonder of wood and gravity
I
Was coaxed into riding that
Rickety monster in the mid-60s
Nearly lost my sunglasses
But
I was chasing a skirt
And well
Viva Skee-Ball!
Her long blond hair
Smelled like fried dough
On finger tips
Mixed with sugar sand
And her strong bikini
Was a cat's cradle
I
Remember the
5-cent changing room
The kiss we shared
There
And the merry-go-round

TEN

CODA

The concluding section of a dance, especially of a pas de deux or the finale of a ballet in which the dancers parade before the audience.

When the flies started falling
like meteor showers
we knew we were in for an ancient horror

By then we were numbly hanging on to
              Nothing
Waiting for the final blow

A clean
immediate death
              Inshalla

Not this creeping
death head virus
Eating like a wild dog
Us

Watch
unable
to so much as
SCREAM

You
Cannot stop them
or die fast enough

Helpless as bay scallops
storm tossed from codium

From spat to spit
              Gone by the next
                        wrack line washed ashore

We are no longer jetsam
More a great gyre of
things we haven't considered

You know Consequences

Contemplation

Tupelo pond
with its bridge
Don
And Andre'
abused
       Ultimately destroyed

Rotten wood rickety
Pond no more than puddle

Two men full of drink
muddled and unrepentant

Murky water floating
Empty beer cans
late model sedan

Too much
for a pedestrian conveyance

Rebuilt with
metal and memories
of two professors'
and a night of bacchanalia
they barely remembered
the next day

The Lost

Long nights spent watching
from a far remove

Sounds of pure delight
Sweat born of ecstatic impetus
        Touch
no more

The calloused hearts
Broken bottles
Shattered conveyances
Abandoned where I fell

The cost of war
for me
        is the lover I never knew

You sing America

I can't
I'm
muted by horrors
that visit me every endless night
        Frozen
in bullet whiz
Cannonade echo

Hold my hand
        Be there when I sleep
if I can

Remain when I wake
if I do

Bring me toast and coffee
Please

Pass the morphine if you
would
I beg you
come closer
I want to come back to you

But this is where I'll remain
       Shaded by a fine copse of trees

Breaking it Down

In the twilight we merge
fang and feather
with muffled leaf rustle
earth hum
night hunger and
creaking floorboards
     in the hour
         that morning comes
For just so long

We'll be eternally
entwined in
one last kiss
Our remnants
will exist
in dust motes
     As always

     Captives of the wind

Oran

The dim-witted character
Camus envisioned reading the Trial
sat down next to me
at the Pig and Whistle
Just around the corner
from my flop

Ordered a day-old floater
and a cup of Joe

Looked around in confusion
for an ashtray

Lit a nail nonetheless
Jaw jutted
Typical inebriate on a bender
His eyes a downed wire
sparking apocalypse for breakfast

Offered me up
one of his Lucky Strikes
like he was brandishing
a switchblade on Broadway

          And I know this is a soon to be
Hopper painting of empty stools

I reach over the counter
grab the bucket of mud
and say

Hey   Death
You want me to top you off

I think we're going to be here
a while

Under an Opossum Moon

I'm a cerulean storm front
riding the smell of rain
      seconds before the first drop heard

Over ripe berry
stain my hands
Pie on the windowsill waiting for a thief
just before the
boom
boom
boom of John Lee Hooker or the
plaintive wail from Joni Mitchell singing Blue

I love you

So
I'll hold my breath
Stop my heart
from beating
bluebells and fare thee wells

Until you come back home

Reference Desk

This is the library
I've always dreamed of
dying in

A flower bed
with blooms
I can count on
returning again and again

long after I'm gone

Someone might pick up
my copy of Gio's book
sitting on the mantle
over the fireplace
long dormant

Sit at my mid-century
Roll-top desk

Read about all the irony
life has to offer

Look at the pictures
and the bric-a-brac
Try to decipher
without the aid
of a proper codex

the husk left behind

Spinning like a ghost on the bottom of a top, I'm haunted by all the space that I will live without you. — Richard Brautigan

Ry

It's on the days when the news is all bad
that I'll remember you best
        Pulling a cork on a bottle

like the first punch thrown in earnest
Never stopped once started

You could spit

in the eye of a daisy
Barking haikus at the
moonfaced and
get away with it

Go
Not misbegotten
Pick up Styx and watch the devil dogs don't
bite your ass

I have your words
right here
in a locket close to my heart

Just the way you wrote it

Miscalculated

Kurt Vonnegut
sued a tobacco company
       Purveyors of "his" brand

The Surgeon General as well
       For breach of promise

A funny thought
       I finally get the disappointment

Seems prognosticators were off
A decade or two
about the final gasps
of humanity

Which leaves this beat up hippie
chin deep in Armageddon

Flabbergasted

It seems like only yesterday
when I could say

I'm glad I won't be here
to see to fruition
all our bad decisions

Certain at Curtains

I will leave you with this
Do with it what you will

This is not so much a manifesto
as it is a valediction – boyo

Run your hands over stone
until it's smooth

Imagine the long dark hallway of a howl

The rest is only pain
          Keep running
You're not going anywhere
on a knife's edge

It's always like that in a dream

If you wake   and I hope you do
search for the pot
of misplaced socks
at the end of your rainbow

Look into the wine dark
          Check for stars

Know as much leaving
as you did on the way in

About the Author

Photo by the late Jim Lentowski, RIP.

Len Germinara has been writing, publishing, and performing his poetry for five decades. For 17 years he ran spoken word venues in Massachusetts from south of Boston to Nantucket featuring some of the best poets in the country including Taylor Mali, Marge Piercy, Gregory Orr, Jack McCarthy, Brother Blue, Steven Dobyns, Franz Wright, Mark Doty and many more.

He currently resides in New England with his wife, Sarah Oktay, two dogs, and a cat. He is on the board of the Sacramento Poetry Center (Emeritus) and is the former host for the Outer Cape radio station WOMR's Poet's Corner. His previous books "Of Course I Could Be Wrong" and "Back Story" are available on Amazon. He has been published in various national journals and publications. For bookings contact him at lensir@hotmail.com. Learn more about him at http://www.lengerminara.com/.

Made in the USA
Middletown, DE
10 August 2023